Keeping Kids Safe

By K. L. Wheatley

Artistic Contributions

Illustrations: Marianne Hallock
Cover Design: Bob Simeone

Leading Edge *Leaders in Child Safety Publications*
Eugene, Oregon

Leading Edge supports all organizations dedicated to children's safety as well as to the prevention, education, and recovery of missing children.

LEADERS IN CHILD SAFETY PUBLICATIONS

Keeping Kids Safe, a comprehensive parent guide, was developed through information gathered from highly regarded safety experts and other organizations that specialize in children's safety. Every step has been taken to supply the public with the most accurate and current information available regarding children's personal safety. However, neither the author nor the publisher assumes responsibility for the validity of all materials or the consequences of their use.

Leading Edge Leaders in Child Safety Publications
Eugene, Oregon

Leading Edge
P.O. Box 70675
Eugene, OR 97401
Phone: (541) 461-9819
http://www.safetykidsclub.com

10 9 8 7 6 5 4 3 2 1

ISBN: 1-891432-01-X
Library of Congress Catalog Card Number: 97-94148

For my son, Morgan; my nieces, Amanda, Taylor, and Alexandra; my nephews, Bobby, Shane, Brent, and Rhys; and all other children; with hopes that they will always be happy, healthy, and stay safe.

Contents

Acknowledgements
Special Thanks
Preface
Introduction

Is Your Child Safe?

What Your Child Needs To Know

How Safe Is Your Child When You Are Away?

Abduction: It's Happening Every Day

More Help For Parents

Keeping Kids Safe

How Safe Is Your Child?

Acknowledgments

Many thanks to all the people who have made this project possible.

Parents: Janet & Craig Ramey, Mitch & Susan Heichen, Chris & Lori Holden, Mary Jane Paul, Charlotte Holden, and Carrie Dewitt; and professionals: Mary French, Ann Stow, Bill France, Lisa Paul, Bill Barton, and Patty Wetterling for their valuable input which gave us the information needed to complete *Keeping Kids Safe*.

Susan Lesyk for her editorial expertise.

Bob Simeone, Marianne Hallock, David Edwards, and Dylan O'Fallon, for their artistic contributions

Connie May Neal, Jamie Snodgrass, Quenton Fraser, Sebastian Fraser, Diana Gasper, and Dean Cupp for their continued support and encouragement.

Alisha Stafford, my right arm; this work would not have been completed without her dedication, personal sacrifice, and knowledge.

A special thanks to my family: My son, Morgan, and my husband, Donnie, who recognized the importance of this project. My brothers and sisters, especially Ricci, who all gave endless hours of effort and heart to this endeavor, and my parents, who have always been supportive and stood behind me.

To the many people who have dedicated their lives to keeping kids safe.

Thank you all so very much!

Special Thanks

Our hearts go out to the many parents who have lost a child due to horrible and tragic criminal acts. Despite the fact that their lives have been disrupted by something so devastating, many of these parents have dedicated themselves to keeping children safe and providing the public with valuable information in order to help the rest of us become child-safety advocates as well. Without their dedication to keeping all children safe, this book would not have been possible:

Maureen Kanka, Patty and Jerry Wetterling, John and Reve Walsh, Kim Swartz, Marc Klaas, Eve Nicol, Colleen Nick & David and Ann Collins

A special thanks to the following organizations whose founders and staff are considered experts in the field of children's personal safety and contributed information to this project:

National Center for Missing and Exploited Children, Jacob Wetterling Foundation, Polly Klaas Foundation, Heidi Search Center, Amber Foundation, and Child Find of America.

For a complete list of Associations and Organizations, please see page 163.

Preface

Every parent has asked the same question that I have struggled with from the moment I became a parent. "How do I ensure my child's safety?" As the mother of a ten-year-old, I constantly found myself with these concerns, but I could never find the answers. I am also an aunt to several nieces and nephews whose parents share these concerns. Where do you find the answers? Unfortunately, there weren't any to be easily discovered. What a shame!

Sadly it became apparent that there was a shocking lack of information available to parents that dealt with children's personal safety. I began to worry about my son's safety and the safety of all children. Since I had so many problems finding the answers on how to keep my child safe, it became obvious to me that **all** parents must be experiencing this same concern. HOW DO WE KEEP OUR CHILDREN SAFE? As a result, I embarked upon a tedious project: To supply information on children's personal safety to as many parents as possible. Therefore I began the grueling process of research.

I cannot begin to explain to you all of the heartaches and absolutely wrenching experiences I had while discovering all of the horrible statistics, circumstances, and real life stories. During my research it became apparent that this was a tragic and prevalent problem *everywhere.* I was saddened by the reality of how unprepared our children and their parents are for the dangers that may affect them. It created a fear within myself that sparked the flame for me to continue. More than anything in this world, I wanted to ensure my child's safety as well as the safety of all children.

Over the past few years, with the help of family, friends, child-safety experts, and many child-safety organizations, we have attempted to compile all the information a parent would need to keep their children safe.

With high hopes and great confidence, I am delighted to present to you **Keeping Kids Safe**, a comprehensive parent guide to children's personal safety.

Our children are our hopes, dreams, and future. Give them the love, **protection**, and self-confidence they need and deserve.

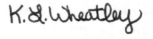

● ● ● ● ● ● ● ● ● ● ○

Introduction

Head down and shoulders heaving, Robert Curley sat hunched on a bench beside the Charles River, sobbing uncontrollably as he asked whether he had done enough to protect his 10-year-old son from murder by sexual predators.

"I agonize over it; I cry over it," Curley said, his head swaying from side to side. "Could I have been a better parent? Maybe there's something I could have done."

"Father of Slain Boy Wrestles with Grief"
Boston Globe, October 17, 1997
by Brian MacQuarrie

Help Your Children Become "Safety Smart."

Crimes against children continue to grow at an alarming rate. Today children are at risk in schools, on playgrounds – even in their own front yard!

But children can do much to protect themselves if they have been properly educated. *Keeping Kids Safe* educates you so you can educate your children. It provides you with the most current information available to help you keep the most precious people in the world safe and secure.

The responsibility for avoiding a tragedy starts not with the children but with you. Don't wait until a tragedy happens, then spend the rest of your life saying, "I only wish I had...!"

"I only wish I had taught her more than - 'stay away from strangers!' "

I

IS YOUR CHILD SAFE?

● ● ● ● ● ● ● ● ● ●   ●   ○

Frightening Statistics

People are suddenly realizing this can happen to them... They don't have to be in the wrong place at the wrong time, and they don't have to be unlucky. This can happen to anyone.

> *Marcella Leach*
> *Justice for Homicide Victims*
> *"Victims' Rights Advocates Urge*
> *Caution in Wake of Tragedy"*
> *Los Angeles Times, April 21, 1997*
> *by Jeff Leeds and Stephanie Simon*

What Are the Odds?

What are the odds of your child becoming one of the many children each year who are abused, abducted or victimized in some way? Small, you say? Think again. Statistics show that it can and does happen, every hour, every day, everywhere. This means it could happen to your child, or to the family down the street. The numbers are rising daily, and the statistics are frightening.

Daily headlines across the country read...

Body of Missing Girl Discovered

Man Confesses to String of Child Abductions

Boy Missing 2 Weeks

Police Suspect Missing Girl Was Abducted

Mother Prays: Search Goes on for Lynn Boy, 6

Molester on Trial in Girl's Murder

Two Missing Children Remain Mystery

The Statistics Are Frightening.

More cases of missing children are reported today than ever before, not only in the United States, but throughout the world. The exact number of children missing throughout the United States each year is unknown; however, the figures most often quoted are between 1.5 and 1.8 million.

The following statistics, released in May, 1990 by the United States Department of Justice and other studies verify the shocking number and types of crimes being committed against our children.

- More than **114,500** attempted child abductions are reported each year.

- **3,200** to **4,600** children are abducted by strangers each year.

- More than **450,000** children run away from home each year in response to neglect and physical or sexual abuse.

- More than **438,000** children are lost, injured, or otherwise missing each year, with 47% of these children under the age of four.

- More than **4,000,000** convicted child molesters live in the United States today.

- **One out of every four** girls will be molested by the age of eighteen.

- **One out of every seven** boys will be molested by the age of eighteen.

- On average, each pedophile violates over **150** children in his/her life.

- More than **40%** of convicted sex offenders who prey on children will become repeat offenders.

...the Federal Bureau of Investigation estimates that approximately four children a day are victims of "stranger abduction."

"After Polly: The Search Continues
for Other Kidnapped Kids"
People Magazine, December 20, 1993
by J.D. Podolsky, Mary Huzinec,
Mary M. Harrison, Nina Burleigh

Determine What Your Child Knows about Safety.

Section 4

Safety Kids Club Safety Test

This comprehensive <u>Safety Test</u> is designed to determine your children's understanding of personal safety. How each child answers these questions will show you the areas that you need to work on with your children to keep them safe.

*This is page 69 of **Kids Keeping Kids Safe**, which has a complete section of friendly tests designed to see what your child really knows about phone safety, strangers, going to and from school safely, and much more.*

What Does Your Child Really Know?

It's everybody's worst fear to think about any kid being placed in danger... As a community, we need to be more vigilant. Students at the school are routinely taught "stranger danger" techniques to defuse dangerous situations...

*David Gavin, Principal
Coronado Hills Elementary School
"Third Kidnap Try in Thornton,
Girl Escapes; Mayor Calls for Calm"
Denver Post, May 8, 1997
by Steve Garnaas and Sheba R. Wheeler*

Is Your Child at Risk?

One of the biggest mistakes parents make today is assuming their children know how to be safe. Developing safety skills at a young age is not something that children just acquire, they need their parents help. If *you* have not taught your children personal safety, *they are at risk.*

For example:

Do you know your children can actually use a pay phone, or do you merely assume that they know how to use a pay phone?

Can your children...

- Operate a pay phone?
- Make a collect call?
- Call long distance?
- Dial 9-1-1?
- Call the operator?

Can your children write...

- Their full names?
- Your full name?
- Their street address?
- Their city and state?
- Their complete phone number, including area code?

Are you sure your children will check with you for permission before...

- Going anywhere with anyone?
- Going into anyone's house?
- Getting into anyone's car?
- Accepting gifts, money, or favors from other adults?

Have you taught your children what to do if they become lost...

- In a store?
- At the park?
- At a theme park or fair?
- At a campground?

Have you taught your children what to do if followed...

- On the way to or from school?
- To a friend's house?
- Through the mall?
- In any public place?

Have you taught your children what to do when on-line and...

- Someone asks them for personal information?
- Someone wants to meet them in person?
- They receive a bad or scary message?

Have you taught your children to "check-in," always letting you know when they...

- Leave the house?
- Go from one place to another?
- Change plans?
- Are running late?

Do your children use the buddy system when...

- Going to and from school?
- Using public restrooms?
- At playgrounds and parks?

Have you taught your children never to play in...

- Isolated areas?
- Abandoned buildings?
- Deeply wooded areas?

Have you taught your children what to do if...

- A stranger asks them for help?
- An adult asks them to keep a secret from you?
- Someone is touching them in a way that makes them feel uncomfortable?

It's Time Parents Educate Themselves

Hundreds and hundreds of children are <u>not</u> abducted, because they are equipped with knowledge...

Anne Cohn Donnelly, Executive Director
National Committee to Prevent Child Abuse
"Child Abductions: What a Mom Must Know"
McCalls, March, 1994
by Carolyn Hoyt

Safety Must Be Taught at Home.

Child-safety experts agree that safety education is critical in today's society. Recently, there have been major cutbacks in school and law enforcement budgets across the nation; therefore, personal safety must now be taught at home.

The **Safety Kids Club "Safety First"** program consisting of **Keeping Kids Safe**, **Kids Keeping Kids Safe**, your **Family Safety Plan of Action**, and the **Personal Records** packet provide your family with the tools to establish an excellent safety program for your family.

What Can Parents Do Today?

- Educate themselves.

- Educate their children.

- Establish family safety rules and procedures.

- Develop a personal *Family Safety Plan of Action.*

- Be advocates for child-safety.

Children Should Feel Safe.

Children should feel safe and know how to stay safe. They must be taught safety procedures, beginning at an early age and continuing throughout their childhood. Begin by teaching your children such things as their telephone number, their full name, your full name, and how to dial 9-1-1 in an emergency.

Learning these safety skills will help children develop self-confidence. Children with self-esteem are less vulnerable and less likely to fall victim to those who prey on children. It is imperative that you start teaching your children basic personal safety skills at an early age.

Do Your Children Know They Can Talk to You about Anything, without Exception?

Talking with Mom or Dad

Safety Rule # 1

Safe Kids know they can always talk to their parents or another trusted grown-up about anything.

Page 45 and following pages of Kids Keeping Kids Safe help reinforce the important idea of confiding in parents.

Communication:
A Safety Must

*The key is communication and self-esteem
... People who victimize children use
subterfuge and seduction. You have to
empower children, so that they have the
right to say no to adults.*

*Peter Banks
National Center for Missing
and Exploited Children
"Divers Widen Search for
Body of Cambridge Boy"
Boston Globe, October 5, 1997
by Peter S. Canellos and Royal Ford*

Establish Good Communication between You and Your Children.

It is critical that your children feel safe and comfortable discussing their problems, fears, thoughts, and dreams with you. Most safety experts agree that children should be encouraged and taught to share their feelings about daily events. This type of communication will help your children continue to share their feelings with you as they grow older.

Children need to feel loved, safe and secure. Positive attention at home will help your children develop high self-esteem.

Help your children get past awkward or uncomfortable topics by assuring them that their feelings are both extremely important and *never wrong*. Let them know you are there to listen and help them.

It is important that you do not get mad or upset at your children even when they are telling you something that is upsetting. These times, although sometimes stressful, provide some of the best opportunities for discussion and learning.

Never act shocked or horrified when your children confide in you. If you do, they might be afraid to tell you about uncomfortable situations they may experience in the future.

Remind them often that your number one concern is their happiness, well-being, and safety. If something is not right with them, you will help them make it right.

Listening to children:

- Create an environment in which your children feel comfortable discussing daily events, bad as well as good.

- Listen to everything your children tell you, no matter how seemingly trivial.

- Never let your children feel their thoughts, fears, or concerns are unimportant, whether they are real or imaginary.

- Help your children understand that many people care about them. They are never alone.

- Explain to your children that if they ever feel a problem is too big for them to handle, they can always talk to you or another trusted adult. They can always count on your support.

- Teach your children that no one should ever ask them to keep a secret from their parents.

- Explain that a "good secret" normally is a present, party, or surprise. Call it a "surprise" rather than a "secret."

- Make sure your children understand how important it is to tell you, or another trusted adult, if anyone makes them feel uncomfortable.

- Encourage your children always to trust their feelings.

• • • • • • • • • • •

Children Need A Positive Self-Image

Child psychologist Russell T. Jones of Virginia Tech institute, known for his research on children's safety, says giving children age-appropriate preventive information about safety is not unlike giving them fire-safety skills. "It empowers a child," he says. "They feel more confident. They think, 'If this did happen, I'd know what to do.'"

"Father of Slain Boy Wrestles with Grief"
Boston Globe, October 17, 1997
by Brian MacQuarrie

Start Young.

A positive self-image is one of the keys to personal safety. Safety experts agree that children need to develop a strong sense of themselves and their family at an early age. Children as young as two-years-old can start learning basic safety skills such as who they are, where they live, who they can trust and who loves them.

Teach your children:

- ❏ Their full name
- ❏ Their full street address, including the zip code
- ❏ Their phone number, including the area code
- ❏ Their birth date
- ❏ Both parents' full names
- ❏ Other family members' full names
- ❏ Extended family members' full names and addresses

Abductors Target Their Victims.

Most molesters and abductors study their victims before committing a crime. They target certain children and then try to win their confidence.

Abductors target children who:

- Are alone
- Appear vulnerable
- Have low self-esteem
- Appear lonely or depressed
- Have problems in their lives
- Have never been taught how to be safe

Teaching your children personal safety is a great way to help build their self-esteem and let them know how special and unique they are.

Help your children to stand tall, be alert, be proud, and be confident of their problem-solving abilities. Give your children the message from the beginning that their lives have great value.

Teach Kids to Trust Their Instincts.

Parents need to help their children listen to their "inner voice." Children who have been taught to trust their first instincts will be safer than children who have not been taught to listen to their "inner voice".

Teach your children not to be tricked into compromising or doubting their feelings. Learning to trust their feelings at an early age will help your child be safe.

Review These Important Safety Concepts Often with Your Children.

Safety Sam's
Safety Kids Club
Top 10 Safety Tips

🐾 Safe Kids can always talk to their parents or another trusted grown-up about anything.

🐾 Safe Kids always "Check First."

🐾 Safe Kids know how to dial <u>9-1-1</u> in an emergency.

🐾 Safe Kids never talk to anyone they don't know well.

🐾 Safe Kids always use the "Buddy System."

🐾 Safe Kids say "No!" to anyone who tries to touch them in a way that makes them feel uncomfortable. Then they tell their parents or another trusted grown-up right away.

🐾 Safe Kids never open the door for anyone but a trusted friend or relative.

🐾 Safe Kids always tell their parents or another trusted grown-up if anyone asks them to keep a secret.

🐾 Safe Kids always follow their **Family Safety Plan of Action**.

🐾 Safe Kids know that their parents would never send anyone they don't know well to pick them up.

*Page 4 of **Kids Keeping Kids Safe** is a concise list of important safety rules.*

II

WHAT YOUR CHILD NEEDS TO KNOW

Beware Of Strangers

*You fear the stranger. The predator. Some-
one with an ice-cold heart and a void soul,
who steals your child, commits
unspeakable violence and then leaves your
child as lifeless as a broken, discarded rag
doll.*

"Predators Strike Fear in Parents..."
Houston Chronicle, April 27, 1997
by Tom Gorman and Jeff Leeds

What Is a "Stranger"?

Webster's dictionary defines a "stranger" as "a guest, visitor, or intruder," or "a person with whom one is unacquainted."

Teaching your children about strangers is one of the most difficult challenges parents are faced with today. You've heard the familiar warnings:

> **"Don't talk to strangers."**
>
> **"Never accept a ride from a stranger."**
>
> **"Don't take candy from strangers."**

In today's complex society, these phrases are insufficient. Give your children extensive "stranger danger" education to ensure their safety.

Patty Wetterling of the Jacob Wetterling Foundation (established after her 11-year-old son Jacob was abducted) advises parents to substitute the phrase "someone you don't know well" for the word "stranger." Children can understand and relate to rules about "someone you don't know well," while they might have trouble determining who is a "stranger" and who isn't.

> **A stranger is any person the family doesn't know well or doesn't consider to be a trusted friend.**

A stranger can be a man or a woman, tall or short, young or old, drive a new car or an old van, be nicely dressed or shabbily attired. In other words, a stranger cannot be described strictly in a visual sense.

Give your children real-life examples of people they don't know well in their own world, such as the pizza delivery person, the person who sells ice cream from a truck in the neighborhood, the neighbor who just walked their dog by the house, and the people in the grocery store.

They (children) think we're saying anybody you don't know is a bad stranger. What happens when Uncle Henry is a dirty old man? ...We have to get off this stranger thing or at least define it.

Robert Stuber, Author of
'Missing! Stranger Abduction'
"Program Helps Kids Escape Abduction"
Houston Chronicle, June 13, 1997
by Stephanie Newton

What Should Your Child Know about "Friends," "Strangers," and "People We Don't Know Well"?

It is vital that you teach your children the difference between a trusted family friend and someone they may see on a frequent basis. Both are easily recognizable to the child, but they cannot be treated the same. "People we don't know well" have to be treated with the same caution we use with "strangers."

Teach your children:

❏ Never help an adult they don't know well. Adults need to ask other adults for help.

❏ Never let someone they don't know well into the house even if they recognize the person.

❏ Never let someone come into the house without a parent's permission.

❏ Never approach or get into a car, truck, or van operated by a person they don't know well-even a *familiar* person such as the postman or newspaper delivery person.

❏ Never go "trick-or-treating," collecting for a paper route, or door-to-door selling without a trusted adult along.

❏ Never accept a free item or gift, such as an ice cream cone, soft drink or any other item. Always "check first" before accepting any item from someone who isn't a relative or close friend, even from a *familiar* person.

❏ Never accept an invitation to go to a neighbor's yard or home without permission. Parents need to know where their children are at all times.

❏ Never talk to casual acquaintances when parents are not present. Seeing people frequently does not automatically make them friends. They are *still people we don't know well.*

❏ To keep a safe distance between themselves and adults they don't know well. If they feel threatened, they need to run to a safe place and tell a *trusted adult* right away.

❏ How to determine "safe people" who can help should a child have an emergency (such as a mother with children or a store clerk behind a counter with a name tag).

Don't Let a Stranger Trick Your Child.

One of the first things children learn to write in school is their name, and they write it everywhere. Having a sense of identity is good, but putting their identity out for the world to see can be dangerous.

Don't let a stranger trick your child by calling out his/her name after seeing it printed on a backpack, T-shirt, or other personal items. Even simple initials can easily be guessed by strangers and give them the opportunity to trick your child.

Don't put your children's names in visible places on notebooks, lunch boxes, bicycles, or sports equipment. Teach them to be suspicious if someone they don't know calls them by their first name and pretends to be a friend.

What if Your Child Needs Help?

The common phrase, "Don't talk to strangers," implies that all strangers are dangerous. But total strangers often come forth in an emergency to save a child's life.

While you are teaching strict rules such as "Keep a safe distance from adults you don't know well," you need to spend time carefully defining an exception to the rule.

Your children must understand that it is **not safe** to help anyone they do not know well who asks them for their help. Adults should never ask children for help.

It is also important that your children understand in an emergency situation who the best people are to ask for help. Give your children some guidelines. Teach them to find a "safe stranger," such as a mother with children, a security guard in a uniform, a school employee, or a clerk behind a counter with a name tag on.

Just because a child does not know a person does not make that person "a bad stranger," because the majority of people in the world are good people... If the child is abducted, or an attempt is made, then getting help from a stranger may be the child's only hope.

Robert Stuber, Author of
'Missing! Stranger Abduction'
"School Watch; Saving Children from Abduction;
Ex-cop Dedicated to Ending Kidnappings"
Atlanta Journal and Constitution, November 20, 1997
by Kay S. Pedrotti

The Difficult Question Remains: How Do We Teach Our Children about Strangers without Scaring Them?

Spend time with your child discussing all the important ideas in *"Kids Keeping Kids Safe."* Children gain self-confidence as they learn to stay with friends, avoid strangers, and share their fears with parents or other trusted adults.

Tricks Predators Use

*What can we as a society do about the
predators who are stalking our children?
Awareness is No. 1. They are out there.
Those who wish to harm children do exist,
and every one of us must be on guard
against them.*

*"Stress Vigilance to Protect Children"
Chicago Tribune, August 13, 1997
by Det. James Cassidy*

What Type of Person Would Do This to a Child?

As parents we would like to have our children grow up believing that the world is a wonderful place. We would like them to feel safe and believe that no one would harm them. Unfortunately, we know this is not the case. Children across the nation are being abducted and molested every day.

Contrary to what most people think, you cannot look at a person and determine whether or not he or she is a predator.

"Predatory" pedophiles are usually males, who may or may not be married with children, and are some of the nicest people you will meet. The stereotype of the dirty old man has nothing to do with who the predatory pedophile is. The predatory pedophile is different from the "incest" pedophile, who sexually preys on youngsters who are his or her own children or stepchildren.

"Youth Service Groups Can No Longer Evade the Threat of Child Abusers in Their Ranks"
by William A. Barton

Predatory Pedophiles Share Common Characteristics.

Although predatory pedophiles may look perfectly normal, safety experts say they usually share some common characteristics.

People who prey on children:

- Prefer children's company over adult company.

- Spend a lot of time with children.

- Lack social skills to interact with adults.

- Usually come from dysfunctional families.

- May have been abused themselves.

- Volunteer or seek jobs working with children.

- Seek relationships with single parents of young children.

- Shower children with gifts.

- Are usually repeat offenders of crimes against children.

Danger Starts with Dialogue.

Safety experts point out that most stranger abductions start with dialogue. Make sure your children know that it is **not safe** to converse with anyone they don't know well. Help them develop the skill to end the dialogue and walk away.

Tricks Work Better Than Weapons.

Most abductors trick children instead of intimidating them with weapons – it's easier and more effective. Abductors know that young children have an innate desire to help people and love the satisfaction and praise they receive for doing something helpful. Asking for a child's help is an effective way abductors can gain control and lure children.

It's difficult to teach your child to be helpful to family and friends yet wary of strangers – but it's not impossible. Learn the tricks predators use so you can teach your children how to guard against them.

"Can You Help Me?"

A plea for assistance is one of the most common tricks used by abductors when preying upon children.

Some examples:

"Would you help me find my puppy?"

"Excuse me, could you show me the way to the police station?"

Questions like these are very effective because children want to be helpful. Some abductors pretend to be blind, hurt, or disabled in order to trick a child into helping them.

Teach your children:

❏ Never to help a stranger with directions. **Explain that adults need to ask other adults for help.**

❏ People with disabilities never go anywhere unprepared; they always have an assistant with them if they are unable to care for themselves.

❏ Never to help anyone they don't know well search for a lost pet.

❏ Never to walk anywhere with someone they don't know well.

❏ Never to get into anyone's car, for any reason, without checking first with a parent or trusted adult.

SOMETHING TO THINK ABOUT

Be conscious of the messages you give, such as asking for help from children you don't know well. Although your requests are innocent, they contradict the rule that adults should ask only other adults for help, not children.

Anthony, his younger brother and two friends were playing behind their homes when a stranger pulled up and offered them a dollar to help find his lost cat.

"Body of Missing Boy, 10,
Found in California Ravine"
Houston Chronicle, April 21, 1997
by Paula Story

"It's Free!"

Abductors often entice children with gifts, while sexual predators use gifts to protect secrets. Children need to be taught that such gifts are bribery. Some examples of bribery might be:

"I have some toys. Would you like to come pick one out to take home?"

"Do you want to go get some candy?"

"Let's go play some video games. I'll pay."

Your children must understand that people who are not trusted family friends should never offer them toys, money or gifts for any reason.

Teach your children:

❏ Never to accept gifts from anyone without checking with you first.

❏ To tell you if an adult is hanging around the neighborhood, school, or play area, offering children gifts or money.

❏ Never to get close enough to a stranger to accept a gift.

"It's an Emergency!"

Abductors might say they have been sent by parents to pick up a child because of an emergency. Examples of the emergency trick or lure include:

> **"Your mom has been hurt, and I need to take you to the hospital."**

> **"Your dad was running late, so he asked me to pick you up."**

Teach your children:

❏ You would never, under any circumstances, send someone they didn't know well to pick them up. You would send only a trusted family friend or relative.

❏ Never to go with someone who has come to pick them up, unless previously arranged by you.

❏ What to do if persons other than trusted adults try to engage them in conversation.

What about a "Code Word"?

Some safety experts suggest using a pre-arranged code word if a substitute must pick up a child, regardless of whether or not the child knows the person. Other experts feel that letting a child have any interaction with strangers is dangerous.

The idea that you would send a **stranger** to pick up your children without letting them know is completely absurd. Therefore, your children should never need a code word. They would know who is supposed to pick them up and know they need to "check first" with a trusted adult if they are unsure for any reason.

Help your children feel comfortable ending or avoiding any dialogue with strangers. Any communication could be dangerous for them.

> *It should be safe for a 9-year-old to walk down the street... It wasn't that day, not for her. There was a predator on the loose. That's what happened.*
>
> Thomas F. Reilly, District Attorney
> Middlesex State Office
> "Pryor's Death Confirmed, Her
> Parents Plan Funeral"
> Boston Globe, January 11, 1998
> by Ellen O'Brien and Mark Brunelli

"I'm a Policeman."

Children are taught that police officers, security guards, and firemen are here to serve and protect. Unfortunately, some abductors pose as authority figures to trick or lure children. Help your children understand authority figures and their duties.

Explain to your children that if they are ever approached by someone looking official who says, "You need to come with me," they should run to a safe place and call 9-1-1 immediately. Assure your children that they will not be in trouble. A **real** police officer will not be upset with a child who uses safety precautions to verify credentials.

Teach your children:

❑ To ask another trusted adult, such as a clerk behind a register, for help verifying that the person with the badge or wearing the uniform is authentic.

❑ Never to leave a building with a person who simply shows them a badge.

❑ Never to get into a car with someone who simply shows them a badge.

❑ How to verify credentials by phone.

❑ Never to open the door for someone who simply shows them a badge.

"Want to Earn Some Money?"

Abductors sometimes trick children by offering them money to do odd jobs around their home or work place. For example:

> "I'll pay you ten dollars to rake all the leaves."

> "Would you like to help me clean out the garage? I'll pay you five dollars."

Teach your children:

❏ To "check first," no matter how big or small the job, even when it is for a trusted friend or owner of a business in your neighborhood.

❏ Never to help strangers load groceries or any other items into their car, even if offered money.

❏ If a stranger offers to pay a lot of money for an easy job, *the person may be trying to trick them.*

"Come with Me, or I'll Kill You."

Not all predators have enough time or skill to trick a child. Instead they threaten children verbally or with a weapon. For example:

"Come with me, or I will kill you."

"I know where you live. Get in the car or I will hurt your family."

Most safety experts agree that the best chance your child has in this situation is to run, yell, attract as much attention as possible, and get to a safe place fast.

Teach your children:

❏ Only a very bad person would scare children by threatening to harm them or their family.

❏ To keep a safe distance away from strangers.

❏ If someone tries to grab them; try to kick, scream, and break away. Run to a safe place immediately.

❏ Even if a bad person has a gun or knife, try to yell and run away.

❏ If they cannot get away from the predator, they should remain calm and look for an opportunity to get away. Assure your child you will find them.

The man asked the children to help him find his lost cat, holding out a dollar as enticement.

"Boy's Kidnapping Unifies Small Town"
Los Angeles Times, April 9, 1997
by Stephanie Simon

Chelsea police had alerted residents Wednesday after a man driving near Park Square tried to lure two 12-year-old girls to his car.

"Chelsea Police, Residents Search
for Missing Girl"
Boston Globe, March 27, 1998
by Mark Brunelli

The pair allegedly lured Jeffrey Curley into a car with promises of a bicycle and $50.

"Father of Slain Boy Wrestles with Grief"
Boston Globe, October 17, 1997
by Brian MacQuarrie

Flicker told the jury that Megan fought back after the defendant lured her into his home... with the promise of seeing a puppy.

"Details Convey Horror of Megan's Death"
Los Angeles Times, May 6, 1997
by John J. Goldman

Puzzles and Cartoons Remind Children to Stay with Friends.

B Buddy System keeps kids safe

Safe Kids know it's more fun to walk with a Buddy, and it's safer too!

My best Buddy to walk home from school with is_____
Other friends to walk with are_____

The ABC's of Safety has several activity pages to help children remember to walk and play with a buddy for safety. This is page 5 of the activity and coloring book.

The Buddy System

We cannot put the responsibility of safety on young kids... It's the parents' responsibility... children (should) use a buddy system and never travel alone...

Nancy McBride, Executive Director
Adam Walsh Center
"Parents, Police Meet on Attempted Kidnappings"
Miami Herald, February 2, 1994
by Rick Dorsey

A Child Alone Is Vulnerable.

Child-safety experts tell us that abductors target children who are alone. Give your children every advantage. The common phrase, "Use the buddy system," is a must in today's society. Children alone have a much higher risk of being in potentially dangerous situations.

Establish a family rule of always using the "buddy system" when your children are young, and when they get older, this habit of staying with friends will remain with them.

Children with positive self-esteem can easily develop social skills and have many friends in the neighborhood and at school. Take the time to help timid children learn how to make friends, which will reduce the chances of them being alone and at risk.

There really **is** safety in numbers. Two heads are better than one, and if one person is hurt or threatened, the other person can help or get help. While two is better than one, three is better than two, four is better than three, etc. The larger the group, the safer your children will be.

Although there is safety in numbers, it is important your children understand that traveling with a buddy does not **ensure** their safety. Your children and their buddies should always follow their personal safety rules. They should never feel that it is safe to talk to someone they don't know well or go anywhere with a stranger just because they are with a buddy.

Teach your children:

❏ Always to use the "buddy system." Walk and play with other children.

❏ Never to go to a park, playground, video arcade, movie theater or public restroom alone.

❏ Never to go out after dark alone.

❏ To form a "buddy group" to walk to and from school.

❏ Never to go door-to-door selling or go "trick-or-treating" in the neighborhood without a buddy. (Don't go door-to-door in an **unfamiliar** neighborhood, even with a buddy.)

Two 11-year-old Springfield girls who were kidnapped Sunday violated a basic safety rule by getting into a car with a stranger... In this case, the girls felt safe because they were together.

> Gwen Anderson, Sergeant
> Lane County Sheriff's Department
> "Casual Decision Proves Dangerous"
> Register Guard, March 24, 1998
> by Eric Mortenson

Help Your Children Remember How to Make Emergency Phone Calls.

M Money is not needed to call 9-1-1

Safe Kids know that in an emergency they can call 9-1-1 or "O" from a pay phone without money!

TELEPHONE

How much money does Zack need to call 9-1-1? $_____

(Fill in the blank)

*This is page 16 of **The ABC's of Safety**. Several other activities in this book and **Kids Keeping Kids Safe** remind children that they don't need money for 9-1-1 calls or calls to the operator.*

Keeping
Kids
Safe

9

Phone Skills
Keep Kids Safe

The phone can be a lifeline for children...

Michelle Ettinger, Relations Manager
MCI Communications
"MCI Launches Telephone
Safety Guide for Children..."
Detroit News, June 25, 1997
by Roshonda Hatley

The Telephone Is a Great Safety Tool.

One of the greatest personal safety tools available to your children is the telephone. Today's technology offers children many ways to communicate, such as home phones, pay phones, cellular phones, pagers, fax machines, and E-mail. Safe kids know that any information or help they may need is only a phone call away.

At a young age your children should begin learning basic telephone skills. These skills develop self-esteem, keep them in touch with loved ones, and keep them safe. Children as young as three-years-old have saved a life by dialing 9-1-1 in an emergency.

You Are Only a Phone Call Away.

Your children need to feel secure even when you are away. Basic phone skills enable your children to reach you at all times. These skills instill security, develop self-esteem, and promote communication between you and your children. Your children will feel safer and more secure knowing that *you are only a phone call away.*

Teach Your Children Basic Phone Skills.

Begin by teaching your children:

❑ Their home phone number.

❑ Their area code.

❑ Your work number.

❑ A trusted friend or relative's number.

❑ How to dial "0" for an operator.

Help your children memorize these phone numbers. Practice using a real phone with your children calling friends or relatives.

Help Is Only a Phone Call Away.

To prepare for emergencies, teach your children:

❑ When and how to dial 9-1-1. Give examples of emergency situations such as a medical emergency, a fire, being lost or afraid, etc.

❑ They can dial 9-1-1 from any phone without using money.

❑ What to say to an operator or a 9-1-1 dispatcher in an emergency. (Make it clear that they must never call 9-1-1 unless it is a real emergency.)

❑ If they need help but don't know where they are or can't talk for any reason, they should still dial 9-1-1. The operator can tell where the phone is and dispatch help.

❑ How to dial "0" for an operator. Give your child examples of situations where they might need help from an operator, such as placing a long distance or collect call.

❑ How to dial home using a pay phone with money and without money.

Today's Technology Makes Communication Easier.

Today's technology broadens our ability to communicate. Your children will be safer if they have been taught how to use all the resources available to them.

How terrible it would be to have a child try to call 9-1-1 on a cellular phone and fail to get help because he/she had not been taught to press "send!"

Teach your children:

❏ How to leave a message on an answering machine and how to retrieve a message from the family answering machine.

❏ How to leave a number on a pager.

❏ How to use a cellular phone.

❏ How to use a business phone that requires access to an outside line.

❏ How to use a hotel phone. Explain that dialing "0" will get them to the hotel operator.

❏ How to use a fax machine.

❏ How to send an E-mail message.

A Caution about Pagers

Some safety experts believe that a pager, carried by a parent or child, won't guarantee a child's safety and might create a false sense of security.

The "Check First" Rule Is Reinforced by Activity Pages.

 Always check first

Safe Kids always check with a parent first before going anywhere. They can have fun and be safe too!

Hey, Mom! Can we go to the park?

Sure, Honey, just be back in an hour. Remember your safety rules!

When should you "check first?" Circle your answers.

Before changing the channel on TV.

Before going to the store with a friend.

Before going to anyone's house.

Before staying after school to get help with your math.

Before playing on the Internet.

*This is page 4 from **The ABC's of Safety**. This book and **Kids Keeping Kids Safe** constantly remind children to "check first" with parents or guardians before going anywhere.*

Keeping
Kids
Safe

• • • • • • • • • • • ○

10

Check First

*Don't let your children go anywhere alone.
Our society is breaking down and you
can't expect kids to watch themselves any-
more.*

*Nancy McBride, Executive Director
Adam Walsh Center
"Robbing the Innocents"
Time Magazine, December 27, 1993
by David Van Biema*

Children Need to "Check First."

Parents need to know where their children are at all times in order to keep them safe. Establish a family "check first" policy. Before your children go anywhere they need to tell you where they are going, who they are going with, how they will get there, who will be supervising, and what time they will return.

It is very comforting for children to know that they are important and that there are safety rules. Often they don't really want to do something friends suggest but feel uncomfortable declining. Saying that they absolutely have to "check first" gives your children a way out.

Make "Check First" Rules Specific.

Teach your children which parent or guardian they should "check first" with. Who else can they "check first" with if you are not available?

Use the **Family Safety Plan of Action** found in **Kids Keeping Kids Safe**. It is the ideal tool for making "check first" rules clear and helping everyone remember them.

Teach your children to "check first":

- ❏ Before going anywhere with anyone.

- ❏ Before going into anyone's home.

- ❏ Before leaving a friend's house to come home or before going to another friend's house.

- ❏ Before getting into anyone's car.

- ❏ Before accepting candy, money, or gifts from anyone.

- ❏ If plans change.

- ❏ If they are running late.

Teach Children to "Check-in" When They Get Home.

It is important that your children understand the urgency of checking in immediately upon arriving at home. This is a family practice that should be established at an early age.

If you don't see them come in, your children are to find you and "check-in" before doing anything else. If you're at work, they must phone you promptly. If they can't reach you or you are not home, have another designated adult prearranged for them to "check-in" with.

Historically, dangers to children were largely physical and often invisible, such as polio. But today, the primary dangers are social and quite visible. Most of the dangers to youth of all ages are people dangers, and they occur most frequently where the children live – in schools, in families and circles of acquaintances and friends.

"Kids Need New Survival Skills for the 90's"
Bill France, Parent Talk

Safety In Your Neighborhood

Cambridge residents... thought their neighborhood was the sort of place where everyone knew everyone and children could safely play outside. But their peace of mind, their security and even their trust in each other was shattered by the double horror of police revelations: Not only had a well-known and outgoing neighborhood boy... been abducted and slain, but one of the men charged with the crimes... lived just around the corner.

"Once Again, a Sense of Community Is Shattered"
Boston Globe, October 4, 1997
by Judith Gaines

Your Child's Independence Begins in Your Neighborhood.

Establish personal safety routines, set definite boundaries, and point out safe places as well as unsafe places throughout the neighborhood.

Teach your children:

❑ To always check with you before going anywhere in the neighborhood.

❑ Which neighbors are trusted family friends.

❑ Which neighbors and homes are to be avoided and which areas are "off-limits."

❑ To "check-in" often when playing in the neighborhood.

❑ To use the "buddy system" when playing in the neighborhood.

❑ To report to you immediately any suspicious persons in the neighborhood.

❑ Not to go door-to-door selling or "trick-or-treating" without an adult along.

Ilene Misheloff, a shy, 13-year-old Dublin girl, disappeared Jan. 30, 1989, as she was walking home from school...

"Amber, Kevin - Other Bay Kidnaps
Remain Unsolved"
San Francisco Chronicle, December 2, 1993
by Kevin Fagan and Michael Taylor

...the stranger grabbed Tony as his 6-year-old brother watched. The man pulled a knife from his waistband and forced the fourth-grader into his truck...

"Boy's Kidnapping Unifies Small Town"
Los Angeles Times, April 9, 1997
by Stephanie Simon

Laura (Smither), 12, vanished April 3 after leaving her home for a morning jog.

"Police Probing Smither Murder to Consult
with Arlington Police"
Houston Chronicle, April 29, 1997
by Ruth Rendon

Polly Klaas, 12, kidnapped at knifepoint from her Petaluma home Oct. 1, was found murdered two months later.

"Marc Klaas, Polly's Dad, to Urge Child
Safety in Session with President"
Chicago Tribune, December 17, 1993
by Katherine Seligman

SUCCESS STORIES

Brooklyn, NY, April 4, 1998 – Two 8-year-old girls were walking down the street after lunch at a pizzeria when a man grabbed one of the girls by the arm and attempted to pull her down the street. The girl tried to break free and at the same time her friend struck the man from behind, who then calmly walked away. Both girls immediately phoned the police!

Houston, TX, March 26, 1998 – An 11-year-old girl was putting books into her family's van in a church parking lot when a predator grabbed her from behind and forced her into the back seat of his car. As he slowed at an intersection about a quarter–mile away, she jumped out and ran into a safe store immediately to phone for help!

Denver, CO, September 17, 1997 – An 8-year-old girl was walking to school when a man driving a van pulled up next to her and asked her if she wanted to go for a ride. She loudly told him "NO!" and ran as fast as she could into the school!

Boston, MA, November, 1997 – An 11-year-old boy was kidnapped outside of his school by a man at gunpoint who then forced the child into a van and drove off. The boy jumped out of the van and escaped when the abductor had to stop in traffic a few blocks away!

WAY TO GO SAFE KIDS!!

● ● ● ● ● ● ● ● ● ● ● ● ●

Safety Away From Home

On Tuesday, two days after the third attempted child abduction in two weeks and the day another was reported in nearby Hometown, Burbank parents sent their children back to school. Along with backpacks and lunches, the children carried warnings about being extra cautious.

*"Abduction Attempts Have Parents
on Edge Over Kids"
Chicago Tribune, August 27, 1997
by Jerry Thornton*

It Only Takes a Few Seconds!

It only takes a few seconds for a child to be abducted. Young children are frequently abducted because one of their parents have left them unattended for just a brief moment. **Never** put your children in potentially danger-ous situations.

To keep your children safe in public:

- Never leave your children alone in public places.

- Never leave your children alone in a car, even if the doors are locked.

- Never leave young children unattended in a grocery cart at a store.

- Teach your children not to wander away from you or play hide-and-seek games.

- When delivering children to a party, class, practice, etc., don't let them off at the curb and drive away. Go in with them to make sure the address is correct, and the event will take place as scheduled.

- Teach your children not to interact with strangers while out in public.

- Help your children identify "safe people."

What if You Become Separated?

Every year thousands of children are separated from their parents when out in public. Most children will experience the feeling of being lost at some point, even if only for a brief moment. Every time you and your children go out into a mall or other spacious and confusing public facilities, make it an opportunity to teach safety concepts.

Help Prevent Panic.

Children who **have not** been prepared for a brief separation and reassured that they will be found immediately will most likely panic and be unable to use good judgment, making them even more vulnerable. Prepare your children by teaching them how to handle this situation and stay safe.

Teach your children what to do if separated:

❏ They should stay calm. This is probably the most important rule. Assure them of your confidence in their ability to make the right safety choices.

❏ Promise them that you will start searching for them immediately. You will not stop looking for them until you find them, even if it seems like a long time to them.

❏ Review your *Family Safety Plan of Action* and the guidelines your family set ahead of time about what to do in this situation.

❏ Designate a meeting spot. If you become separated, they are to go there.

❏ Discuss the dangers of your children wandering around looking for you or leaving the building. If there is no designated meeting place, they must stay where they are.

❏ Explain to your children never to leave the area with anyone, even if the person says he or she will take them home.

❏ Remind your children they can dial 9-1-1 in an emergency. An operator will help them decide what to do.

❏ Encourage your children to look for "safe people" if they need help.

"Safe People" who can help:

• A store clerk with a name tag.

• A cashier at a cash register.

• A security officer in a uniform.

• A police officer in a uniform.

• A woman with children.

Keeping
Kids
Safe

● ● ● ● ● ● ● ● ● ● ● ●

13

Safety When Alone

There's not a day that goes by when people don't think about the families and the girls that lost their lives... It's so scary because the girls were abducted from right in front of their homes. As parents, we've all told our kids to stay away from strangers and not get into anyone's car. But in a situation like this, what can you do or say?

Donna Steinberg, PTA president
Spotsylvania High School
"With Killer at Large, Va. County Is Rewriting
After-School Rules..."
Washington Post, September 7, 1997
by Leef Smith

Section II • What Your Child Needs To Know   77

Is Your Child Ready to Be Left Alone?

There are many factors involved in determining when a child is ready to be left alone. There is no magic age. You must consider each child's maturity, phone skills, problem-solving abilities, and general safety smarts. How safe is the neighborhood? How close are friends and relatives?

Most states have laws that set specific **minimum** age requirements for leaving children alone. Check with your state to see what specific age requirements apply. Most safety experts advise parents to **never** leave a child under age 10 alone.

It is up to the parents to determine when their children are mature enough to stay at home alone. In many situations, it may not be safe to leave even a 13 or 14-year-old child alone.

Most important, make sure your child feels safe and comfortable alone.

Before leaving them alone, teach your children:

❏ Not to let anyone know they are home alone.

❏ Not to let anyone in the house when they are home alone.

❏ To keep doors and windows locked at all times.

❏ Not to leave the house without calling a parent or responsible adult first.

❏ To "check-in" with a trusted friend or relative when you are unavailable.

How Safe Is Your Child on the Bus?

Many children take the school bus while other children use public transportation. Remember that each child is unique and special, some children may not be ready to take on the responsibility of riding the bus alone. It is an age–appropriate activity and each parent should decide when their child is ready and prepared to ride the bus safely.

Many children are approached daily at school bus stops and public bus stops across the country by predatory pedophiles. It is important that you teach your children the precautions they need to take and to be aware of their surroundings while waiting for the bus.

When your children use public transportation, teach them "safe people" to sit by – such as the bus driver or a woman with children. Explain that these people are still "people they don't know well," but they are the best choice.

Don't encourage a child to sit too far away from others because an empty seat next to a solitary child is an invitation to a predator.

Establish Your Family Safety Plan of Action.

Children should not be left alone unless a *Family Safety Plan of Action* has been established. This personalized plan allows you and your children to set individual safety guidelines.

A complete *Family Safety Plan of Action* should include:

- Emergency numbers and where they are posted

- General family safety rules

- Family safety rules to follow when home alone or with a baby-sitter

- Safety rules to follow when going to and from school

- Prepared scripts for answering the telephone and door

- How to handle any emergency situation

- Who your children should call if you are unavailable

- Specific rules to follow while on the Internet

Develop Your Family's Safety Plan of Action.

Section 3

Our Family Safety Plan of Action

*You'll find the help you need outlining your family's rules in the **Family Safety Plan of Action**, found on page 56 in **Kids Keeping Kids Safe**.*

Safety To And From School

The Wednesday evening rally and march marked the one-year anniversary of Jaycee Lee Dugard's kidnapping. It happened as she walked to the school bus stop... Her stepfather... watched in horror from the family garage a third of a mile away...

"California Album; the Kidnapping No One Will Forget... "
Los Angeles Times, June 12, 1992
by Dan Morain

Determine a Safe Route.

Walking to and from school is one of the most dangerous situations for children today. **More children are abducted on their way to and from school than under any other circumstance.** Your children will not be able to protect themselves from dangerous situations unless they have been taught proper safety techniques.

Safety experts advise parents to walk the route with their children - not just once but frequently.

Point out the following:

- Places to avoid

- The correct side of the road to walk on and locations of crosswalks *(Many experts recommend walking on the sidewalks **against** the traffic.)*

- Who "safe people" are on their route, such as crossing guards and trusted neighbors

- "Safe places" they can go to for help, such as retail stores, restaurants, library, fire station, safe homes, etc.

Establish to and from School Safety Rules.

Parents must take extra precautions to ensure the safety of their children when going to and from school. You must determine a safe plan.

This plan should include:

- What route your children will take
- How long it takes them to walk the route
- Who your children will walk with
- Dangerous places to avoid
- Places they should be extra careful
- Safe places to use a phone
- Safe places to get help

If approached by someone in a car, your children should:

- Step away from the car. Do not be tricked or lured to come closer, even by a "hard of hearing" person.
- Avoid getting into a conversation with the stranger.
- Take a few steps back and get ready to run in the opposite direction of the car.

If a stranger threatens, your children should:

- Do everything to get away, even if the person has a weapon. Ignore the weapon and run.

- Not worry about personal items. Throw books and bags down and get away fast.

- Yell loud and clear, and attract attention from anyone who is nearby.

- **Never** get into a car. While on the street running and yelling, a child has a chance to escape. A child who is pulled into a car may have no chance.

- Get to a safe place as fast as possible – a public place, **not** an isolated area.

Does Your Child's School Have a "Call-Back" Program?

Most schools have set up a "call-back" program, which means they call parents if a child does not arrive at school so a search can begin immediately. Make sure schools have alternate phone numbers in case they are unable to reach you at home.

If your child is ill or not in school for any other reason, call the school as soon as possible.

Check with your child's school to make sure there is a "call-back" program. If not, join other parents in urging that one be set up. Many schools use volunteers to work in the attendance office during the morning.

In a missing children's case, Etan Patz, a first-grader from New York, didn't show up at school one day. The school failed to notify his parents of the absence until the end of the school day. Etan remains missing today.

When Children Are in Trouble, Yelling Might Be the Only Thing That Saves Them.

 Yell if you need help

Yelling is an important safety tool
Safe Kids can use in emergencies.

When should I yell as loud as I can, and when
should I stay cool? Circle the best answer.

Yell   Stay cool   My little sister keeps taking my toys.

Yell   Stay cool   A stranger tries to make me go in a car
                      with her. She tells people she is my aunt.

Yell   Stay cool   My mom won't buy me candy when we are
                      at the store.

Yell   Stay cool   I am lost in the woods,
                      and I know people are
                      looking for me.

Yell   Stay cool   Our team makes a big
                      score!

Yell   Stay cool   A weird guy is trying to
                      make me go into the
                      restroom with him.

*This is page 28 from **The ABC's of Safety**. It gives you a
chance to discuss with your children when it's appropriate for
them to yell as loud as they can.*

How To Yell For Help

You don't want to create too much fear in children, but you have to educate them... We tell school students that if anyone drives up, they should scream and run in the other direction. That usually scares them off.

Vincent Taylor, Police Lieutenant
"Divers Widen Search for Body
of Cambridge Boy"
Boston Globe, October 5, 1997
by Peter S. Canellos and Royal Ford

Children Must Let People Know if They Are in Trouble.

Most people would help a child in trouble. However, if they do not realize that the child is in distress, they cannot help. How many times have you seen a child being carted out of a store crying? In the past, most adults assumed the child was just acting up. Now we should consider that the child might be in danger.

Your Children's Voices Are Their Emergency Alarms.

Today parents must realize how important it is to teach their children to yell – and **what** to yell – in a dangerous situation.

Experts tell us that most abductors will leave children alone if they draw attention to themselves by yelling, kicking, and screaming. Their voices are their emergency alarms. Here are some guidelines to keep your children safe.

Teach your children:

❏ Never to be embarrassed to yell for help.

❏ To yell *"Help me!"* with a strong, confident voice.

❏ If a stranger or bad person is forcing them to go somewhere, they should yell, *"This is not my mom!"* or *"This is not my dad!"*

❏ It's okay to say **"NO"** to an adult in an uncomfortable situation.

Play "what if" scenarios with your children to practice saying "No!" or "Help me!" Make sure your children feel comfortable running if they are in a dangerous situation.

Children Need Special Training to Say No to Adults Who Are Acting Inappropriately.

*Page 49 of **Kids Keeping Kids Safe** teaches children to resist unwelcome contact with adults.*

How To Say No

*Young children can be talked into lots of
things because they do not have the ability
to reason that they are being manipulat-
ed. Everything is concrete to them.*

Dr. Paula Jorne, Therapist
"Special: Public Safety: Pedophiles
Can Hide Under Many Guises..."
Detroit News, November 18, 1997
by Brian Harmon

Children Have the Right to Say "No."

Your children must know that they are special – *and they have rights!*

Your children should feel comfortable greeting a relative with a hug or a kiss, and expressing natural feelings of affection. Give examples to your children of who should give them affection, and that a hug or kiss from a loved one, like grandma, is okay. However, they are not *obligated* to hug or kiss anyone if it makes them feel uncomfortable.

Explain to your children that their bodies belong to them, and they have the right to say, "NO!" Teach your children alternative ways of saying "No!" For example: "Please do not hug me," or "I do not like it when you kiss me."

Help your children understand that a caring relative would not be offended if they do not feel comfortable showing affection.

Communication is a family's most important safety tool. Your children must feel comfortable reporting to you any feelings of discomfort. Remind your children that they can always talk to you about anything.

Teach your children:

❏ No one has the right to make them feel uncomfortable. They should tell a parent immediately if anyone makes them feel uneasy.

❏ There is a difference between a "good touch" and a "bad or uncomfortable touch."

❏ Their bodies belong to them.

❏ They can say "No"– politely at first, then loud and clear.

❏ They don't have to hug or kiss anyone if they don't want to.

❏ The parts of their bodies that are covered by a bathing suit are "private parts."

❏ The proper names of their private parts.

❏ No one has the right to touch their private parts.

❏ No one should ever ask a child to touch anyone else's private parts.

*For safe fun on the Internet, or more
information on the topics covered in this
book and others, you can contact us at
http://www.safetykidsclub.com
or call us
Toll-Free: (877) Be-A-Safe-Kid
Local: (541) 461-3362*

● ● ● ● ● ● ● ● ● ● ● ●

Safety On The Internet

*The Internet has been a dream come true
for a pedophile... It has taken the playground from the street and put it into
their home where they can cultivate potential victims in secrecy and in seclusion.*

*Paul Reid, Police Detective
"Sexual Predators Lurk On-Line,
Congress Told: Officials Say Internet
Offers Direct Line to Kids"
Chicago Tribune, November 8, 1997
by Tamara Lytle*

What Is the Internet?

Millions of computers are linked electronically on a worldwide network, the Internet. Even people who don't have a computer can use the Internet at schools and libraries.

With the Internet you can communicate with people all over the world. You can send E–mail to a specific person or carry on a running conversation with several others in a "chat room." You can post a message on a "bulletin board" for anyone to see. You can order tickets, download software, or get information from almost any large company, government agency, or organization.

What Are the Risks to Children on the Internet?

As computer technology makes its way into homes across the country, we are beginning to hear reports of children being lured and victimized through the Internet. While there are many advantages to the resources that the Internet provides your child, there are many dangers.

On the Internet, your children can chat with pen pals from all over the world. They can also chat with predators. For example, a 38-year-old sex offender can easily pretend to be a 9-year-old girl who likes video games. Help your child understand that things are not always as they seem.

Dangers of the Internet:

- Children viewing sexual materials
- Children viewing violent materials
- Strangers tricking children into giving personal information or sending pictures on-line
- Children being lured into dangerous situations
- Children receiving inappropriate or threatening messages

Help Keep Your Child's On-Line Activities Safe.

Discuss the positive and negative aspects of on-line services with your children. Explain that when using the Internet, like any other activity, safety precautions must be followed. As a family, develop a *Family Safety Plan of Action* for on-line safety.

As a parent, you need to:

- Explore the Internet on your own.
- Spend time with your children when they are on-line. Have them show you what they do.

- Make the use of the Internet a family activity. Keep the computer in the living room or family room, not in a child's bedroom.

- Set rules about how often the computer can be used; discourage late night use.

- Be cautious of using the computer as a baby-sitter, and don't let it substitute for real life friends.

- Monitor the web sites your child views. Know how to find the "history" of sites visited, and check it periodically.

- Discuss the positive and negative aspects of on-line services with your children. Explain that safety precautions must be followed.

- Develop a *Family Safety Plan of Action* for using the Internet.

- Check with your service provider or a computer consultant about software available to block out indecent material.

Teach your children:

❏ Never to give personal information on-line, such as their name, address, phone number, age, sex, name or location of school, or any daily activities.

❏ Never to send a picture of themselves or give a physical description to anyone.

❏ Not to arrange a meeting with anyone they meet through the Internet without having a parent present. (Even then, have the first meeting in a public place.)

❏ To tell parents immediately about any bad messages, anything that makes them feel uncomfortable or scared, or anything which simply does not feel right.

Report disturbing incidents to your Internet service provider.

Much has been made of the potential hazards to children in cyberspace. Chat rooms that might expose young computer users to pedophiles and Web sites with inappropiate material are very real dangers.

"Missing Linked"
Times-Picayune, February 4, 1997
by Staff

CyberTipline Launched to Combat Child Sexual Exploitation on the Internet

"We stand together united in our commitment to make the World Wide Web a safe place for children to explore and learn, without the threat of victimization... Ensuring that our children's Internet on-line experiences are safer and more rewarding is a high-level priority as more and more families go on-line. This CyberTipline is a critical step toward enhanced child safety. It empowers parents to take immediate action and it compliments the industry's position of "zero tolerance" for the exploitation of children using this medium. All of us in the Internet community are committed to the Tipline's success."

Plans for the CyberTipline were first announced by Vice President Gore last December at the Internet On-line Summit: Focus on Children in Washington, D.C. The Tipline was created for parents to report incidents of suspicious or illegal Internet activity, including the distribution of child pornography on-line or situations involving the on-line enticement of children for sexual exploitation. To make a report, simply visit the Center's website at http://www.missingkids.com/cybertip or call your report into the Center's toll-free 24-hour tipline at 1-800-843-5678.

Press Release from NCMEC, March 9, 1998

III

HOW SAFE IS YOUR CHILD WHEN YOU ARE AWAY?

Working With
A Baby-Sitter

*One of two young sisters kidnapped in
Michigan by their former baby-sitter was
molested as many as three times during
the five-day ordeal... The girls' former
baby-sitter has a juvenile record for sexual
assault.*

*"One of Two Sisters Was Molested
After Abduction, Detective Says"
Houston Chronicle, March 27, 1997
by Mike Schneider*

Be Cautious When Choosing a Baby-sitter.

Leaving your children in someone else's care can be difficult. Take your time and find the right sitter. Thoroughly check references such as past employers, other neighbors, or parents. Ask them about the sitter's qualifications and ability to care for children.

Many parents don't think to ask the sitter for important information such as their full name, home address, telephone number, driver's license number, and social security number.

Discuss Your Family Safety Rules.

Don't put your children in danger by assuming that a baby-sitter knows proper safety procedures. Safety experts recommend that you review family safety procedures with the sitter.

Be sure your baby-sitter knows:

- Your *Family Safety Plan of Action*.

- The phone number where you can be reached.

- Your children's allergies and special health needs.

- What medications your children may be taking; review the dosages.

- The emergency phone numbers, including medical offices (leave signed consent forms in case of a medical emergency).

- The phone number of a relative or friend who will be available in an emergency.

- Your prepared phone script such as "_____ cannot come to the phone right now. May I take a message?"

- The locations of thermostats, fuse box or circuit breakers, light switches, first aid kit, and flashlights.

- The fire escape route.

Explain that you expect your baby-sitter to:

- Never let your child go anywhere with anyone, unless previously arranged by you.

- Keep all doors and windows locked.

- Never open the door for anyone unless previously arranged by you. If a person in authority (such as a police officer) comes to the door, carefully check credentials.

- Never leave your children unattended, especially when they are outside playing.

While you are away:

- Phone the sitter to make sure everything is okay.

- Talk with your children to make sure they know where you are and feel comfortable with the sitter.

- Call immediately to give the sitter any new phone numbers if you change locations.

When you return home:

- Discuss activities or events that occurred while you were away. Did anything unusual happen?

- Talk with your children about their feelings regarding the baby-sitter. Discuss likes and dislikes and determine whether they felt comfortable with the sitter.

- Determine whether your children were safe. Talk to trusted neighbors about what they observed.

Choose a Good Baby-sitter, and Teach Your Children Their Responsibilities.

Our Family's Safety Rules to Follow When Home with a Baby-sitter

1. _____

2. _____

3. _____

4. _____

5. _____

6. _____

7. _____

We Promise... To follow our family's safety rules when we are with a baby-sitter.

_____
(Sign your names here)

*Work up specific family safety rules for your children and baby-sitters with page 61 of the **Family Safety Plan of Action**, part of **Kids Keeping Kids Safe**.*

Working With Your Child's School

The nearly simultaneous disappearances of two Washington area children, one from the yard of a Prince William County home and the other from his District school, have provoked an outpouring of anguish from parents and child care providers who say the cases remind them that young children are vulnerable – even in places where they're supposed to be safe.

"Parents Ask, 'What if It Were Mine?'"
Washington Post, October 24, 1996
by Jacqueline L. Simon

Carefully Choose a Pre-school or Day Care Center.

Choosing a pre-school or day care center for your children is tough these days. Parents' number one concern is the safety of their children. Research shows that children are generally safe at most accredited facilities. To further assure your child's safety, do your own homework. Safety experts recommend the following guidelines.

Guidelines for choosing a facility:

- Verify that it is a licensed facility.

- Check the facility's reputation with your local police, Better Business Bureau, Chamber of Commerce, and Children's Services Division. Have any complaints been registered?

- Ask for references from other parents who have used the facility.

- Make sure management has set employee standards for:

  a. Educational background

  b. Emotional and mental stability

  c. Ability to work with children

- Make sure management has reviewed employees' references and police records to rule out:

    a. Alcohol or substance abuse

    b. Incidents of sexual abuse

    c. Incidents of physical abuse

- Avoid day care centers that do not allow parents to drop in unannounced, at any time throughout the day.

- Avoid centers that have areas "off limits" to parents.

- Check the known registered sex offenders file on the Internet or with local police.

Be Involved at Your Child's School.

Your children spend a large percentage of their time in school. Whether your children are in pre-school, kindergarten, elementary, middle school, or high school, *make it a top priority to get involved.*

Get to know all teachers and administrators well. Be sure they know you and your children. Today many schools encourage parents' participation through volunteer programs such as parent helpers, class parents, field trips, holiday parties and other activities.

Help assure your child's safety at school:

- Get to know employees, volunteers, and anyone else who will be interacting with your children.

- Establish in writing who is allowed to pick up your children. Make it clear that no one else, **under any circumstance**, is allowed to pick them up without your written authorization.

- Check to make sure the school has a call-back program to notify parents if children do not arrive at school.

Detecting Sexual Abuse

A federal appeals court Wednesday declared New Jersey's Megan's Law constitutional... The law is named for their 7-year-old daughter, Megan (Kanka), who was murdered in 1994 by a sex offender who lived in their neighborhood. The family didn't know the man had been convicted twice of sexual attacks on children.

*"N.J.'s Megan's Law Upheld: State
Can Warn of Sex Offenders"
USA Today, August 21, 1997
by Bonna M. de la Cruz*

Know the Warning Signs of Sexual Abuse.

As terrible as it seems, children are being sexually abused every day. Safety experts suggest that parents watch for these warning signs in order to help a child who may be in trouble.

Extreme change in behavior:

- Sudden bouts of crying
- Moodiness
- Depression or withdrawal
- Aggression or rebelliousness
- Stress or unhappiness

Changes in sleep patterns:

- Nightmares
- Bed-wetting
- Fear of going to bed
- Fear of sleeping alone

Physical changes:

- Pain or itching in the private area
- Bleeding, fluid, or rawness in the private area

- Sudden interest in sexual matters:
    a. Inappropriate behavior
    b. Acting out sexual activities
    c. Knowledge of sexual matters

Other symptoms:

- Lack of interest in situations normally thought of as fun
- Infantile behavior

Listen to your children. Find out the reason why a child may not want to be at a particular place or with a certain person. There is always a reason why a child is upset.

Parents need to be aware of adults in your child's life who may be showering them with gifts or paying an unusual amount of attention to your child.

If you suspect sexual abuse...

Take your child to a trusted family physician immediately.

Child molesters can be very smooth, very caring, very generous and very dangerous to your children. Many will take months to cultivate your child, gradually reducing their natural resistance to their unnatural and ungodly sexual advances.

> Clinton R. Van Zandt
> Retired FBI agent
> "Spotsylvania Parents Hear Warning of
> Continued Danger"
> Washington Post, May 18, 1997
> by Eric Lipton

Less than 2 percent of the child sexual abuse cases reaching the Snohomish County Prosecutor's Office involve strangers to the victims…. In 97% of the alleged child sexual abuse cases which reach the prosecutor's office, the suspected adult is acquainted with or related to the child.

> "Children Need to Learn Rules
> for Handling Sex Predators"
> Bill France, Parent Talk

IV

ABDUCTION: IT'S HAPPENING EVERYDAY

Family Abduction

*Six-year-old Buster Howard never really
knew his father and hadn't seen him in
five years until he showed up at the boy's
Plainfield home last Friday, saying he
wanted to be the father the boy hadn't
known.*

*Two days later, the father... took the boy
to a park and never returned... and police
have been searching for the blond, blue-
eyed boy and his father ever since.*

"Dad Sought in Plainfield Boy's Abduction"
Chicago Tribune, June 27, 1997
by Jerry Thornton

Abduction Is an Increasing Problem.

Family abduction has become a major problem in the United States and is increasing daily. According to a 1990 report from the Department of Justice, 354,000 children are abducted by non-custodial family members each year.

Unfortunately, experts tell us most parental abduction is done out of vengeance toward the other parent, not out of love for the child.

Are Your Children at Risk?

If you are concerned that your children are at risk of being abducted by an ex-spouse or family member, plan ahead. Safety experts recommend these guidelines:

a. Obtain legal custody of your child. Keep certified copies of the court order ready to show authorities.

b. Compile information on your ex-spouse:
   - Full name
   - Address
   - Phone number
   - Birth date
   - Social Security number
   - Drivers license number

- Primary occupation

- Work number and address

- Photographs

- Physical description (height, weight, hair color, eye color, glasses, distinctive identifying features such as scars, tattoos, ear or other body piercing)

- Names, addresses and phone numbers of close friends and family

- Any medical condition that requires medication on a maintenance basis

c. Obtain passports for your children. Notify authorities that your children are not to leave the country with anyone but you.

Prepare Your Children.

If they are at risk of family abduction, remind your children you are the parent who is responsible for taking care of them. They may spend time with the other parent, but they belong with you.

Extra safety precautions to take:

- Reinforce your family safety rule of always checking in.

- Make sure your children know you will always love them.

- Reassure your children that you will always want them and would never stop searching for them if they were lost or missing.

- Discuss "what if" scenarios with your children and options for contacting you if they are taken. Teach them to look for opportunities to get to a "safe place" and call 9-1-1.

- Make sure your children have memorized your full name, phone number, and address. They should know how to write you as well as call you.

While her mother watched in shock, 3-year-old Andrea Danille Johnson Ray was abducted Saturday from her Idaho Springs home by a woman authorities believe was acting on behalf of the child's father.

Kathleen Johnson stood nearly paralyzed as the woman grabbed her child, then handed the little girl over to a man identified as... the child's father...

"Dad Suspect in Abduction of 3-year-old"
Denver Post, August 11, 1997
by Ginny McKibben

How To Recognize
A Child In Trouble

*On December 4, 1972, 7-year-old Steven
Stayner was walking home from school.
Two men in a car told him they were collecting money for the church. He agreed to
show them the way to his house.*

*For the next 7 years, Steve grew up as an
abducted, sexually abused child. Some
people knew, but didn't do anything. Some
suspected, but would not get involved.
Most people didn't see the signs that could
have saved him. And so it went on.*

*The Steven Stayner Story
Jacob Wetterling Foundation*

How Can You Help?

Start by making a personal commitment to help keep all children safe. Adults have a civic as well as moral responsibility to help ensure the safety and well-being of all children.

Keep Your Eyes Open.

Many families have been reunited because someone sensed that a child's living situation was not quite right. Media resources, such as TV, the Internet, newspapers, magazines, posters, flyers, advertising mailers, and the Executive Memorandum of Missing Children, give hope for the safe return of our missing children.

> *In 37 percent of kidnapping cases, we found witnesses who saw the killer with the child but didn't realize it... Most people don't perceive the danger or that an abduction is going on.*
>
> *Dr. Robert Keppel, Chief Criminal Investigator*
> *Washington Attorney General's Office*
> *"Study Says Megan Slaying Fits*
> *Pattern for Such Cases"*
> *New York Times, June 23, 1997*
> *by Robert Hanley*

You Can Make a Difference.

Keep your eyes open. You may be the one to make the critical phone call which rescues a child.

March 1997 • Thanks to a conscientious nurse, Jedd is home safely.

Jedd's photograph was recognized by a nurse who had previously treated him for a broken arm, and she called the police.

April 1997 • Thanks to a neighbor, Shane is home safely.

In Copper's Cove, Texas, Shane's picture was featured on a poster on a Wal-Mart bulletin board. A neighbor recognized her and called the police.

November 1997 • Crystal is safe now, thanks to the person who reported that the girl was being abused.

Seven years after Crystal was kidnapped from her bed in San Diego, California, police in San Juan, Puerto Rico investigated a citizen's report that a girl was being abused. They recognized her from the National Center for Missing and Exploited Children's web site which displays current pictures of missing children at http://www.missingkids.com.

Recognizing a Child in Trouble.

When should you investigate or report suspicions to authorities? It's a hard decision to become involved in someone else's family life. The Jacob Wetterling Foundation urges you to trust your instincts for any family situations that do not seem right. It gives these guidelines:

A child who's been abducted:

- Often lives with a single man who is passing as the father or grandfather.

- May have changed physical appearance, such as dyed or cut hair.

- May have an overprotective parent who keeps very close tabs on the child's activities and friends.

- May not remember the other parent.

- May exhibit inconsistencies relating to names, birth dates and past events.

- May seem fearful of law enforcement.

- May seem fearful of the parent or guardian.

- May have academic problems and seem withdrawn or neglected.

If You Suspect a Child Is in Trouble, Take Action.

If you suspect that someone is a child abductor, or you have spotted a missing child, call the *National Center for Missing and Exploited Children* or call the local police.

Do not talk yourself out of it. Your call may be the child's only hope.

Provide this information:

- Description of child
- Description of adult
- Where sighting occurred
- When sighting occurred
- Description of vehicle and license plate number

National Center for Missing and Exploited Children
1-800-THE-LOST
All sightings can be kept confidential.

Signing of Executive Memorandum of Missing Children

Every parent knows that their children are the most important thing in their lives. We cherish them, we invest our hopes in them, and when they fall victim to harm, it can be the most wrenching experience of all. For every parent, one of the most horrible things imaginable is the disappearance of a child. We must do whatever we can to help parents in these situations find their children.

We must do everything we can to stop this from happening again. Time is the enemy in abduction cases – and the most important tool we have against it is making sure information gets out to the public.

Today, I will sign an Executive Memorandum directing all agency heads to take the necessary actions to allow the posting of photos of missing children in federal buildings. This presidential action also directs agencies to appoint an action officer to maintain the space for these notices.

… Every one of us must take responsibility to do what they can to help find our missing children. Please look twice at the photos of missing children you see…

President William Jefferson Clinton
Oval Office
January 19, 1996

Thousands of Children Are Missing.

On the following pages are pictures of eight children who are currently missing. If you have information about any of these children, please call the **National Center for Missing and Exploited Children** at 1-800-THE-LOST.

To review more pictures of missing children, you can run a search on the Internet under "missing children", or go to the National Center for Missing and Exploited Children's web site at http://www.missingkids.com.

National Missing Children's Day is May 25.

At six-years-old   Age progression to
                          8-years-old

Morgan Chauntel Nick

Race and sex: White female
Date of Birth: 09/12/88
Hair: Blonde
Eyes: Blue

Identifying marks: 5 visible, silver caps on
    molars. She was last seen wearing a green
    Girl Scout shirt, blue denim shorts and
    white tennis shoes.

Circumstances: At 10:45 p.m. on June 9, 1995
    in Alma, Arkansas, six-year-old Morgan
    Nick was abducted from a little league
    ballpark by an unknown white male. She
    was attending a game with her mother and
    had joined some friends to catch lightning
    bugs. Morgan was last seen standing near
    her mother's car where she had stopped to
    empty sand from her shoes.

Zachary Ramsay

Race and sex: Black male
Date of Birth: 12/18/85
Hair: Brown
Eyes: Brown

Identifying marks: He has a scar between his
eyebrows and on his arm. He has blotchy
skin and dimples. Zachary is biracial; Black
and White.

Circumstances: Child was last seen in Great Falls,
MT leaving his residence for school at about
7:30 a.m. on February 6, 1996. He did not
arrive at school and has not been seen or
heard from since.

Karen Rosalba Grajeda

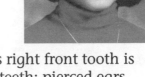

Race and sex: Hispanic female
Date of Birth: 10/15/88
Hair: Brown
Eyes: Brown

Identifying marks: Karen's right front tooth is
larger than her other teeth; pierced ears.

Circumstances: Last seen January 11, 1996 in
Tucson, AZ playing outside in front of her
apartment complex. Karen disappeared
and has not been seen since.

Kirsten Hatfield

Race and sex: White female
Date of Birth: 2/12/89
Hair: Brown
Eyes: Brown

Identifying marks: Kirsten has a mole on her
    left cheek.

Circumstances: The child disappeared from her
    bed sometime between 11:30 p.m. on May
    13 and 6:30 a.m. on May 14, 1997, in
    Midwest City, OK. A small amount of blood
    was found at the scene and her underpants
    were found in the backyard.

Sabrina Aisenberg

Race and sex: White female
Date of Birth: 6/27/97
Hair: Brown
Eyes: Blue

Identifying marks: None.

Circumstances: Child became missing from her
    residence in Valrico, FL sometime during
    the early morning hours of November 24,
    1997. Her yellow blanket is also missing.

Jesus de la Cruz

Race and sex: Hispanic male
Date of Birth: 1/3/90
Hair: Brown
Eyes: Brown

Identifying marks: Jesus has a scar above his left eye and a birthmark on his left calf and on the left side of his forehead. His left ear is pierced.

Circumstances: Child was last seen walking on Park Street in Lynn, MA on September 28, 1996.

Brittney Beers

Race and sex: White female
Date of Birth: 8/1/91
Hair: Blonde
Eyes: Blue

Identifying marks: She was wearing a white tank top, bright pink shorts, and white shoes. Her front four teeth are missing.

Circumstances: She was last seen playing outside of the Village Manor Apartment complex in Sturgis, MI on September 16, 1997.

At eleven-years-old

Age progression to
nineteen-years-old

Jacob Wetterling

Race and sex: White male
Date of Birth: 2/17/78
Hair: Brown
Eyes: Blue

Identifying marks: Mole on left cheek.

Circumstances: On the evening of October 22,
1989 in St. Joseph, Minnesota, Jacob
Wetterling was abducted by a masked man
with a gun while returning home from a
convenience store. A half of a mile from
the Wetterling's home, Jacob, 11, his
brother Trevor, 10, and a friend Aaron, 11
were riding their bikes home after picking
up a movie, when a masked man came out
of a driveway, ordered Trevor and Aaron to
run into the woods or he would shoot them.
As Aaron and Trevor reached the wooded
area, they turned around again and the
gunman and Jacob were gone.

Your Child's Personal Records

Law enforcement officials say time is a critical factor in rescuing and saving children who have been kidnapped... The ability to quickly alert citizens and neighboring law enforcement agencies... vastly increases the chances of making a quick arrest and saving the child.

"Saving Children"
Houston Chronicle, December 12, 1997
by Staff

Keep a "Personal Records" Packet on Hand.

My child is missing! The thought is inconceivable. Unfortunately, one day it could be a reality.

Time is critical. Parents must be prepared to assist law enforcement and other agencies with the most current, accurate information possible.

Safety experts advise parents to compile a complete *"Personal Records"* packet for each of their children. Keep them in a safe, easily accessible location.

Documents and information to include:

- Birth certificate
- Passport
- Full name
- Nick name
- Nationality
- Fingerprints
- Height
- Weight
- Eye color
- Hair color
- Current photos

- List of distinguishing marks or identifying features (scars, moles, birthmarks, pierced ears, glasses, etc.)
- Regional accent or unusual speech patterns
- Medications that must be taken on a regular basis
- Names, addresses, and phone numbers of dentist, pediatrician, and family doctor

Fingerprint Your Child.

Your child's **Personal Records** packet should include an official set of fingerprints. Around the country there are many service clubs, businesses, and government agencies which provide fingerprinting service as special events or as an on-going service. There is usually no charge.

Call your local police department or sheriff's office. If they do not provide finger-printing services, they can probably refer you to another organization that does. If not, call Safe Kids Inc. at (877) Be-A-Safe-Kid.

What If Your Child Is Missing?

Luis Melendi's legs buckled. His wife dropped to her knees to pray. Family members had told them their daughter, Shannon, was missing. Immediately, Luis Melendi knew she had been abducted.... That Sunday evening two weeks ago, Luis and Yvonne Melendi entered a nightmarish world understandable only to other parents whose children are missing.

> *"Child Is Gone, Nightmare Begins; Family Clings to Hope While Searching for Daughter"*
> *Sun-Sentinel, April 10, 1994*
> *by Don Melvin*

What Should You Do
if Your Child Is Missing?

If your child should become missing, the **National Center for Missing and Exploited Children** suggests the following:

Call the police immediately:

- Identify yourself.
- Disclose the location you are calling from.
- Report that your child is missing and request an officer be sent immediately.

While waiting for the police to arrive:

- Search the house and yard thoroughly.
- Check with neighbors.
- Check with your child's friends.
- Notify a security officer or the store manager if you are out in public.

Information to give police:

- Provide police with a current photograph and vital personal information about the missing child immediately. If you have compiled the **"Personal Records"** packet, with information listed on pages 142-143, you can hand over everything instantly.

In addition, provide such information as:

- Location last seen
- Description of clothing
- Unusual circumstances

Request that your child be entered immediately into the National Crime Information Center (NCIC) Missing Person's File.

Don't Let Your Child Leave the Country.

If you suspect non-custodial parent abduction, call immediately to halt issuance of a passport. Have orders that your child is not to leave the country.

Have a Packet of Personal Records Ready to Assist Authorities in Case Your Child Is Missing.

Safety Kids Club
Personal Records

Child's full name_____

Nicknames_____

Address_____

City_____State____Zip_____

Telephone_____

Social Security Number_____

Birth date_____Sex: M F

Envelope Contents:

_____Medical information   _____Current photographs

_____Parent information   _____Fingerprints

_____Birth Certificate   _____Social Security card

_____Vaccination records   _____School records

_____Copy of custodial papers (if parents are divorced)

This packet was updated:	Location of duplicate records:	Date duplicate records updated:

*It's easy to assemble and maintain all the records on your children with the "**Personal Records**" packet, part of the **Safety First** program.*

V

MORE HELP FOR PARENTS

Keeping
Kids
Safe

The Safety Kids Club

Your family will enjoy learning personal
safety procedures with our read-together
parent/child activity books full of tips to keep
kids safe! The *Safety Kids Club* will help you
teach your children personal safety awareness.

Kids Keeping Kids Safe is an 80-page book
which teaches your children safety skills in a
positive and fun way. Your children will build
self-esteem while learning safety skills with
Safety Sam and the *Safety Kids Club*. *Kids
Keeping Kids Safe* helps prepare your child for
situations that could become unsafe or uncomfortable.

Children will be eager to learn any topic if you make it fun. That's why the **Safety Kids Club** activity books have cartoons and puzzles. As your children work with the materials, discuss their answers, praise them, laugh with them, and hug them. If they associate safety books with pleasant attention from parents, they'll want to pick them up often and review them on their own.

Though the format is friendly, the message given throughout **Safety Kids Club** materials is very serious. It may save your child's life.

The Safety Kids Club helps you teach your children:

- How to avoid unsafe situations
- How to detect danger signs
- How to get help if necessary
- How to get out of uncomfortable situations
- How to stay safe

Look for "Teaching Moments."

Concepts taught constantly in small doses are much more likely to be remembered than those taught occasionally in long sessions. Keep **Safety Kids Club** materials handy, so they are available when an opportunity to teach arises.

Teach safety whenever you can:

❑ When your child comes home from school

❑ At meal times

❑ Riding in a car

❑ On public transportation

❑ At bedtime

❑ During "family night"

❑ Anytime

Use Imaginative Teaching Techniques.

Teach safety rules as many different ways as you can, as often as you can.

How you teach depends on several things – the age of the child, whether you have one child present or many, and whether you have a minute or an hour. Even a one-minute quiz might provide a concept that sticks and saves your child's life.

Use games whenever possible. Pick certain topics, such as "strangers," and personalize it by playing "what if" and guessing games, using examples of familiar people and places.

Safety Games That Reinforce Safety Rules.

"I'm thinking of..."

You think of a mystery person, place, or thing. Children solve the mystery by asking questions which you answer with "yes" or "no." This is basically the old "twenty-questions" game, but children should get the answer with three or four questions, after which you can discuss why the answer is correct. Examples:

- "I'm thinking of a neighbor who would help if you got hurt when I wasn't home."

- "I'm thinking of a place you could call if I had already left work but was late getting home."

- "I'm thinking of a person at your school who knows our whole family well."

"Safe or Unsafe?"

Give each child a green card with the word "Safe" written on it and a red card with the word "Unsafe."

Present a situation in which there are two possible answers, pause a moment, then say **"Safe or Unsafe?"** Children give their answers by holding up the green or red card.

Some examples:

"Good surprise or bad secret?" The red card means "Bad secret–must tell!" Holding up the green card means "Nice surprise–don't tell." Examples:

- "Pretend I'm a baby-sitter: 'Don't tell your mom I took pictures of you when you were taking a bath'... Safe or Unsafe?"

- "Pretend I'm Grandma: 'Don't tell Grandpa that I'm going to have a surprise party on his birthday'... Safe or Unsafe?"

"Friend or someone we don't know well?" Green means "Safe–Friend or family, we can trust this person." Red means "Unsafe–Stranger, or someone we don't know well." Examples:

- "The man who mows our lawn... Safe or Unsafe?"

- "The school secretary... Safe or Unsafe?"

- "Uncle Roger... Safe or Unsafe?"

- "The paperboy... Safe or Unsafe?"

> *You can adapt many common games to teach safety concepts or make up your own. They don't need to be fancy; they just need to be done frequently. You must review often because children forget, people move, and situations change.*

Get More Safety Kids Club Materials.

You have just completed *Safety Kids Club "Keeping Kids Safe*," a comprehensive parent guide to children's personal safety. In addition to the parent guide, *Safety Kids Club* materials include *Kids Keeping Kids Safe*, which was developed to be the accompanying parent/child read-together personal safety activity book.

You and your children will enjoy learning together as you complete the activities in the children's book. *Kids Keeping Kids Safe*, the heart of the *Safety Kids Club*, is written on a child's level. It is an on-going personal safety program divided into the following four sections:

ALL ABOUT ME AND MY WORLD

This section gives your children an understanding of who they are, who their parents are, where they live, and the special people in their lives. It is designed to help your child build self-esteem and develop a strong sense of family.

SAFETY RULES

Safety Sam and his friends introduce personal safety rules in a way that makes learning fun. For each lesson there is a brief story, with *Safe Kids* reminding children about safety rules. Personalize each topic with "what if" games, using examples of familiar people and places to help your child fully understand each safety guideline.

FAMILY SAFETY PLAN OF ACTION

This section provides your family with a personal *Family Safety Plan of Action.* You and your children will feel safer after developing your family's individual safety rules.

SAFETY TEST

A comprehensive *Safety Test* helps determine your child's understanding of personal safety. The *Safety Test* is designed to get honest answers from each child. How your children answer these questions will help you determine which areas you need to work on.

Remind your children that they can always talk to you or another trusted friend about anything. Help them build their self-confidence by encouraging and praising them throughout each chapter. Talk about the ideas often – at meals, when you travel, when you tuck them in at night, whenever you can.

Recommended Reading

Tears of Rage

This is the powerful story of Walsh's transformation from grieving father to full-time activist, and how he enlarged the search for Adam's killer into an exhaustive 16-year battle on behalf of thousands of missing and abused children.

By John Walsh with Susan Schindehette, 1997

"I've never really spoken about these things to anyone before, but I want to talk about Adam before he died. I want people to know just exactly how horrible it is to lose your child, how painful it is. But I also want to talk about how people can help you and how you can help yourself. About how to come to terms with life when you think you're dying of a broken heart."

– *John Walsh*

Special Acknowledgment

Every parent is indebted to John Walsh, who used his influence to make protecting children a high priority in the United States.

Since his son Adam was abducted and murdered in 1981, he has worked tirelessly to teach parents how to protect their children from predators, to promote cooperation among police departments and the FBI, and to advance legislation to protect children.

He has spent the past 16 years diligently working to further the campaign to raise national awareness of the crimes committed against children. In the beginning his efforts were focused on putting the faces of missing children on milk cartons. Since then he has fought for the passage of the federal Missing Children Act, the founding of the **National Center for Missing and Exploited Children**, and the enactment of hundreds of state and local laws.

These actions have sparked an international awareness of a very frightening and horrific reality: Predatory pedophiles and those who wish to harm children do exist. They walk the streets each and every day, looking for another child to violate.

His popular TV show, *America's Most Wanted*, has been responsible for the recovery of many missing children and the punishment of their abductors. John Walsh continues to fight this battle with hopes of ending all crimes against children.

Associations And Organizations

Adam Walsh Children's Fund, FL
(800) 892-7430; (561) 863-7900

Amber Foundation for Missing Children, CA
(800) 541-0777; (510) 222-9050

Child Find of America, Inc., NY
(800) 426-5678; (914) 255-5706: FAX

CyberTipline, VI
(800) 843-5678
http://www.missingkids.com/cybertip

Child Quest International, Inc., CA
(888) 818-4673; (408) 287-HOPE
http:/ /www.childquest.org

Child Search National Missing Children Center, TX
(800) 832-3773; (281) 350-KIDS
http://www.childsearch.org

Child Trace International, Inc., KS
Home DNA Identification Kit
(800) 235-2574; (954) 561-6330
http://www.peaveycorp.com

Child Watch of North America, FL
(800) 928-2445; (407) 290-5100
http://www.childwatch.org

Children of the Night, CA
(800) 551-1300; (818) 908-4474
http://www.childrenofthenight.org

Children's Rights of America, Inc., GA
(800) 422-4673; (770) 998-6698
http://www.cra-us.org

Exploited Children's Help Organization (ECHO), KY
(502) 458-9997; (502) 458-9797: FAX

Find the Children, CA
(888) 477-6721; (310) 477-6721
(310) 477-0731: FAX
http://www.findthechildren.com

Heidi Search Center, Inc., TX
(800) 547-4435; (210) 650-0428
http://www.halcyon.com/alt.missingkids/

Iowa's Missing and Exploited Children, Inc., IA
(712) 252-5000

Interstate Association for Stolen Children, CA
(916) 631-7631

Jacob Wetterling Foundation, MN
(800) 325-HOPE; (320) 363-0470
http://www.jwf.org

Laura Recovery Center Foundation, TX
(281) 482-5723

Lost Child's Network, MO
(816) 361-4554

Missing and Exploited Children's Association, MO
(410) 667-0718; (410) 282-0437

Missing Children Help Center, FL
(800) USA-KIDS; (813) 623-5437
http://www.800usakids.org

Missing Children Minnesota, MN
(888) 786-9355; (612) 521-1188

Missing Children Center, Inc., FL
(407) 327-4403

Missing Youth Foundation, NE
(800) 52-FOUND

Morgan Nick Foundation, AR
(501) 632-6382

Mothers Against Drunk Driving, TX
(800) 438-MADD; (214) 744-6233

National Center for Missing and
Exploited Children, VI
(800) THE-LOST; (703) 235-3900
http://www.missingkids.com

National Clearinghouse on Child Abuse
and Neglect, VI
(800) 394-3366; (703) 385-7565

National Crime Prevention Council, D.C.
(202) 393-7141: FAX

National Domestic Violence Hotline, TX
(800) 799-7233; (512) 453-8117
http://www.inetport.com/@ndvh

National Missing Children's Locate Center, OR
(800) 999-7846; (503) 257-1308
http:/ /www.cybernw.com

National Organization for Victim Assistance, D.C.
(800) TRY-NOVA; (202) 232-6682

National Resource Center on Domestic Violence, PA
(800) 537-2238

National Victim Center, VI
(800) FYI-CALL; (703) 276-2880
http://www.nvc.org

National Victim's Constitutional
Amendment Network, D.C.
(800) 529-8226
http://www.nvc.org/nvcan

Nation's Missing Children Organization, AZ
(800) 690-FIND; (602) 944-1768
http://www.nmco.org

Nevada Child Seekers, NV
(702) 458-7009

Office for Victims of Crime Resource Center, MD
(800) 627-6872

Operation Lookout National Center
for Missing Youth, WA
(800) 782-7335

Paul and Lisa Program, CN
(800) 518-2238; (860) 767-7660
http://www.paulandlisa.org

Polly Klaas Foundation, CA
(800) 587-4357; (707) 769-1334
http://www.pollyklaas.org

Rape, Abuse & Incest National Network
(RAINN), D.C.
(800) 656-4673
http://www.rainn.org

Resource Center on Domestic Violence, Child
Protection, and Custody, NV
(800) 527-3223

Services for the Missing, Inc., NJ
(609) 783-3101

Sexual Assault Support Services, OR
(800) 788-4727

Vanished Children's Alliance, CA
(800) VANISHED; (408) 296-1113
http://www.vca.org

Keep Them Safe!

Childhood is a precious time that comes just once and is quickly over. Don't let any child's life be ruined by the predators who have invaded our society.

Hug your children, have fun with them, and keep them safe so they can enjoy all their growing-up years!

Parents, the following information is available upon request.

❏ More lures or tricks that strangers use

❏ On-line safety

❏ Fingerprinting my child

❏ New laws

❏ Sex offenders in my area

❏ How to help find missing children

❏ How to become an independent agent or distributor

❏ Safety seminars in your area

Safe Kids Inc.

You can call us toll-free at
1-877-BE-A-SAFE-KID
or write us at
**Safe Kids Inc.
1574 Coburg Rd., Ste. 141
P.O. Box 70597
Eugene, OR 97401**

Also, visit us at our web site:
http://www.safetykidsclub.com

Safety

Program Price List		
Product	Price	Freight
Safety First	$29.95	$4.95
ABC's of Safety	$3.95	$1.95
Kids Keeping Kids Safe	$8.95	$1.95
Keeping Kids Safe	$15.95	$2.95

(Prices are subject to change depending on consumer location.)

Give the gift of safety!

Product:_____ Quantity:____

_____ ____

_____ ____

_____ ____

Freight charges: _____ Total enclosed: _____

SHIP TO:

_____

_____

_____

(Please use street address.)

TO ORDER, Call:
Toll-Free: (877) Be-A-Safe-Kid

Local: (541) 461-3362

or Fax: (541) 461-3364

or send check or money order to:

Safe Kids Inc.
1574 Coburg Rd., Ste. 141
Eugene, Oregon 97401

We accept: